# STEAM MEMORIES: 1950's - 1960's

## No. 43: East Coast Main Line Part 2

*Book Law Publications*

## Introduction

The second part of our ECML journey takes us from Peterborough to Retford, via the famous Stoke bank, down which MALLARD 'flew' on her record breaking run in 1938. The long gone station at Essendine is our first stop for it was here that junctions from Bourne and Stamford joined the main line. Various wayside stations are viewed en route to Grantham, our first major traffic centre on this section. Pausing at Grantham, a railway crossroads from the start with lines heading eastwards to Lincoln and Boston, and westwards to Nottingham, our trek continues. Peascliffe tunnel momentarily hides the wide vistas of the Lincolnshire countryside from our view but then comes Barkston triangle, followed by Newark where the Midland line from Nottingham to Lincoln crosses on the level. On now to Tuxford where the former LD&ECR main line from Chesterfield to Lincoln crossed the ECML at a higher level. So, to our next stop – Retford. Here another flat rail crossing occurred, as the Great Central line from Sheffield to Lincoln bisected the Great Northern main line. Two engine sheds were to be found at Retford, both having long ago closed but, while one was demolished, the former GNR shed managed to cling on into the 21st century. The flat crossing has been replaced by a dive-under but Retford remains as an intermediate stop on the way north from King's Cross, and it is here where this section of our journey comes to an end.

*Neville Stead, Whitley Bay, 2011*

*(Title page)* **The view northwards along the former Midland Railway (Leicester line) adjacent to Spital Bridge signal box on Friday 18th July 1958. A Nottingham-based Stanier 8F No.48614 is working a southbound coal train from Toton to Whitemoor. In the middle background, with plenty of steam to spare and lots of coal in their tenders, two V2s wait to relieve the motive power of northbound ECML workings. On the horizon Westwood bridge spans the two main lines and the approach/departure lines of Westwood and other yards. Note the two sets of concrete segments marking the openings to a redundant, and dilapidated, air raid shelter beneath the embankment.**

*Printed and bound by The Amadeus Press, Cleckheaton, BD19 4TQ.*
*First published in the United Kingdom by Book Law Publications, 382 Carlton Hill Nottingham, NG4 1JA.*

Peterborough (North) station, Monday 12<sup>th</sup> June 1961. The 9.49 a.m. York-King's Cross rolls into platform 2 as it slows for the last stop before London. A3 No.60047 DONOVAN looks spick and span in the bright but hazy midday sunlight, even the buffer heads are clean but probably none of the waiting passengers nor the station staff will have noticed. They have more important thoughts – such as goodbyes, getting a seat, the journey ahead, getting the luggage and mail loaded, not to mention making sure the train gets away on time.

This elevated view of the southern end of Peterborough (North) station on Wednesday 23rd July 1958 reveals much of interest. Firstly we have the New England based Ivatt Cl.4, No.43086, at the head of a service off the M&GN line; this was to be the final summer for the M&GN as British Railways were about to start a programme of line closures, the likes of which had never been experienced. The station here had seen the birth of the M&GN and was about to see its demise too. Except for platform extensions and the addition of further waiting rooms in GNR days, the station is little changed from its opening in August 1850. Various schemes to rebuild, modernise, and even replace the GN station had been proposed during its existence but plans were thwarted for one reason or another. Indeed, the track layout had necessitated a 20 m.p.h. speed restriction until after the end of steam working and it was 1972 before the alignment was radically altered for the better. The adjacent Great Northern Hotel on the right of the picture was opened in 1851; the GNR making a statement to all and sundry, and especially the Midland Railway, that Peterborough was their patch. To the left of the station are the through lines and the former Midland route, the latter's Spital Bridge engine shed can be seen in the distance with its coaling plant towering above the yard. The M&GN closure in February 1959 brought change to Spital Bridge shed and the reduction in its locomotive allocation set the wheels in motion for its closure too. As for the Ivatt Cl.4 - No.43086 started and ended its days at New England shed. Delivered new from Darlington in November 1950, it was transferred to Melton Constable in June 1957 but returned to Peterborough three months later. With much of its former workload now gone, the 2-6-0 re-allocated to March in December 1960. In July of the following year it moved to Cambridge for an eleven month stint prior to going back to March. In September 1962 Lincoln took it on and managed to keep it busy until January 1964 when it was sent back to New England. Its end came, when it was condemned, during the following December.

Two engines were shunting stock around Peterborough (North) station on Wednesday 23rd July 1958. A scruffy looking N5, No.69290 with an O target board, and long-time New England resident C12 No.67398 which presented a cleaner though far from pristine exterior. The C12 was the station pilot that day whilst the six-coupled tank was collecting and sorting various pieces of rolling stock around the area. The N5 was a newcomer to Peterborough, its transfer to New England from Tyne Dock having taken place just ten days before it was caught on film performing these duties. Its stay lasted until the end of the year when it was re-allocated to Darnall, swapped for sister No.69292. No.67398 had been at New England for just eighteen months but it did not see out the end of 1958 as it was condemned when called into Doncaster works in November. A regular feature of railway stations at this period was the presence of numerous Service personnel en route from one posting to another. Most were conscripts but many, including the two NCOs approaching the camera, were professional soldiers or airmen. The other 'feature' in the frame was the trainspotter, this one wearing a raincoat, the deep pockets of which were useful for notebooks, pencils and sandwiches.

Another N5, this time No.69293, approaches Spital bridge with a miscellany of coaching stock on Friday 18th July 1958. This one came to New England during the previous April from Chester, ending a sixty-three years association with engine sheds in Cheshire and Lancashire. This engine is tidying up the station area and taking advantage of a lull in the traffic to make a short foray up to the yards north of Spital. It is worth studying this and similar illustrations in this album which were taken from the same bridge on the same afternoon – the coming and goings are almost perceptible. The N5s arrived at New England to work the Stamford-Essendine mixed passenger/goods trains and to take over the station pilot and shunting duties at Peterborough from the remaining C12s. This engine never returned to its native Gorton and was condemned at Doncaster works the end of November 1960 and cut up there.

Copley Hill A1 No.60130 KESTREL enters Peterborough (North) with the 7.52 a.m. express from Leeds to King's Cross on Monday 12th June 1961. This particular summer was to prove the last one when express passenger trains were mainly in the hands of steam locomotives. The first diesel locomotives had made their appearance on ECML expresses in 1958 and it had been a slow transition to get them all diesel hauled but by the end of 1961 the English Electric Type 4 and Deltic fleets were growing in numbers. However, the winter of 1962-63 found the diesels wanting, so steam made a swift, albeit short, comeback to main line passenger working between London and Edinburgh. Once the warm weather returned, the summer of 1963 brought about the withdrawal of many former LNER Pacifics, although this particular A1 was not amongst them and managed to remain in traffic until condemned in October 1965.

We now feature B17/6 No.61605 LINCOLNSHIRE REGIMENT passing Peterborough North Box whilst in charge of an unknown Up passenger working circa summer 1952, when it was allocated to March shed. In the latter years of the decade, March engines worked to Leicester and Rugby via Peterborough so perhaps this is one of those trains (albeit in 1952). No.61605 kept the original BR emblem until it went for scrap in 1958; its last 'shopping' prior to being condemned was at the end of 1955, before the later BR crest was brought into use. It was a Stratford engine both before and after the stint at March shed.

A quick look at Spital Bridge engine shed yard circa September 1955 reveals one of the depot's D16/3s which had arrived in 1953 from Cambridge. Their presence at the former Midland shed was to work the passenger services to Leicester, Northampton and Rugby. No.62551 is turned, coaled and ready for its next working to Leicester. The GER 4-4-0s were no strangers to Peterborough; indeed this particular engine had spent ten years at the former Great Eastern shed at Peterborough East from 1929 to 1939 during which time it had been rebuilt from D15/2 to D16/3. Now approaching fifty years of age, the engine was just about ready for retirement. A refurbished boiler fitted in July 1955 did not help to stave off the inevitable and it was condemned at Stratford in July 1956.

Going back in time to Saturday morning 25th March 1950, we see one of the more usual occupants of Spital Bridge engine shed in the shape of long time resident 3F No.43319. The fifty-eight year old 0-6-0 is being serviced and some poor devil can be made out in the pit beneath raking out the ash pan. The look on the face of the young cleaner/fireman in the cab seems to be one of relief that this is one engine he didn't have to get beneath. Perhaps the smokebox char awaits his attention! This Johnson 3F was withdrawn at Derby in December 1950. They seem to have liked the old 'uns at Spital Bridge. Before the decade was out, Spital Bridge itself was run down ready for closure in the first month of 1960. Demolition of the roundhouse soon followed and the landmark coaling plant was reduced to a pile of broken concrete and twisted steel.

In July 1958 this was the kind of activity taking place on the south side of Spital bridge. Here we find a northbound express negotiating the 20 m.p.h. dogleg whilst departing North station with New England's A2/2 No.60505 THANE OF FIFE in charge. Looking remarkably clean for a 34E engine, the Pacific had just over a year of operational life left before it was condemned. Another New England charge, J6 No.64265, waits patiently for the express to accelerate away so that it can continue to New England yard with its mixed train of empty wagons. The 0-6-0 would outlive the Thompson engine by nearly two years before it too was broken up at Doncaster. Through the heat haze it is just possible to make out a diesel multiple unit standing at North station's platform 6. Sweeping across the picture to the right we have the Midland's main line flanked by sidings on either side. The Down line is clear except for a train receding in the distance but the Up line appears to be in use for wagon storage; more than likely the train is being split whilst there is a lull with through traffic. Spital shed's mechanical coaling plant surveys the scene, and although very much in working order, its days were numbered. What a cracking picture recording not just a moment in time but a whole era.

A final look at the southern vista from Spital bridge on that Friday 18th July 1958. A few hours have passed and it will be noted that wagons, or rather trains of wagons have moved on, the Midland lines are clear for through traffic once again and the rake of coaches stabled by the Engineer's premises have also gone. A sort of 'clear the decks for the weekend' has taken place but that was not necessarily the case because the railway scene here changed by the hour, as was the nature at busy junctions. It is early evening now as W1 No.60700 (a regular on this particular heavy working) negotiates the dog-leg with the 4.05 p.m. King's Cross to York/Leeds express. Waiting for its path behind the passenger train, an unidentified but well turned-out A4 heads the King's Cross-Niddrie (Scotch Goods) fast freight. It's time now to move on from Peterborough but before we head northwards to Essendine we must call in at New England shed.

New England engine shed gained some modicum of fame – or infamy, depending on your views – when a fair number of Thompson Pacifics of Class A2 and its sub classes were allocated there during the BR years. Of course the singleton (thankfully) A1/1 No.60113 was also allocated to New England in BR days but only for a short period from 4th June 1950 to 9th September 1951. Three of the A2/2 arrived in time for Christmas and New Year 1949/50 but these had been preceded by five A2/3 in 1948. Amongst them was A2/3 No.60523 SUN CASTLE seen on the east side of the shed yard circa August 1958. The BR crest on the tender is one of the wrong (i.e. right hand) facing examples which would have been applied during a General overhaul in early spring of 1958, just before BR corrected their heraldic blunder. No.60523 had three stints at New England; the last one, from 23rd September 1962, saw it condemned and eventually despatched to Doncaster for scrapping less than a year later. Behind the engine is the old erecting shop in which Sturrock hoped to create the GNR's main locomotive works but after the creation of Doncaster 'Plant' works, New England became merely a satellite works, albeit carrying out heavy repairs and boiler changes but on a much lesser scale than the Yorkshire establishment. SUN CASTLE is actually stabled on one of the tracks which once gained access to the workshop – through the tall double doors – and onto a traverser which ran along the inside, middle bay of the building from left to right (south-west to north-east) as we view it here. The workshop layout was remodelled towards the end of WW1 and the traverser replaced to run south-east to north-west, also inside the shop. To cater for re-siting the new traverser, a new entrance for locomotives was created (this was covered and allowed the electric traverser to work outside of the shop to pick-up its charges) approximately half-way along this wall of the building – directly behind 60523's smokebox – and the aforementioned tall doors became redundant but were not, as can be seen, removed.

Enough of the 'glamour.' Presented here at New England is the last former Midland & Great Northern Railway locomotive in service, and the only one to get the British Railway 60000 number (13<sup>th</sup> November 1948). J4 No.64160 was also the only one to get a General overhaul during BR days (4<sup>th</sup> October to 15<sup>th</sup> November 1948 at Doncaster). Looking rather dilapidated here, the 0-6-0 may have been photographed during 1951 prior to its final visit to Doncaster, an event which took place in late November – it was condemned 3<sup>rd</sup> December. Rebuilt from J3 to J4 in 1937 during a Heavy overhaul at its first Doncaster visit, the engine was renumbered into the LNER system as 085. It kept that number until the Thompson renumbering scheme of 1946 was implemented and it became 4160 on 13<sup>th</sup> August 1946 at New England shed, its home since 16<sup>th</sup> August 1938 after a move from South Lynn. Prior to the LNER taking over the M&GN system and its locomotives, this engine was maintained by the small works at Melton Constable which had looked after it since its October 1900 delivery from Dübs. This view at the south end of the shed yard shows part of the original shed in the background and, of course, the yard prior to the erection of the water gantry which spanned the shed roads from the 1952 rebuilding of the shed.

Essendine – Junction for Stamford and Bourne. We are now eighty-eight miles from King's Cross and the ECML at this location is a four-track formation with three of the through lines serving the station platforms – Up slow, Down fast, and Down slow – the Up fast passed through unobstructed. At first glance (if you ignore the surrounding green pastures) this place could be set in the suburbs of north London. However, we are in deepest Rutland at a place created by the Great Northern Railway in July 1852 in order to connect their main line with the once important town of Stamford (which we will visit later) via a branch line, and, via another branch just south of the station, the market town of Bourne located approximately six miles to the north-east. We are looking southwards and the nearest platform is the Down slow which was used by the branch passenger trains from the aforementioned places. The date is 16th May 1959 and one of New England's recently acquired batch of N5, No.69292, appears at the head of a rather short goods train waiting for the off. Besides working these lightweight goods trains, the N5s also worked the Stamford passenger services, effectively replacing the ex GN C12 4-4-2 tank engines. During the early 1930s the LNER put in the large water softening tower seen on the right of the picture. This lofty structure fed a 30,000 gallon tank, just visible behind it, which in turn supplied the water columns on the platforms and in the goods yard. The sidings were laid down during World War Two; their main function was to stable trains delivering ammunition to the nearby RAF ammunition depot at Park Farm. The GNR had built a small goods yard and shed on the east side of the station (the shed actually out of frame to the left) to handle the local goods requirements. The population here, even in late LNER times, never exceeded three hundred souls and, with the eventual demise of the branches, there was no longer a need for the station. Essendine closed in June 1959.

During the British Railways period passenger services between Essendine and Stamford (East) on average numbered six return trips daily with seven on Saturdays, about half of the pre-war frequency. This is a Stamford train leisurely awaiting a main line connecting service at Essendine in May 1959 shortly before the branch to Stamford, along with Essendine station, closed. By now the former GNR station at Stamford had closed and services from Essendine ran into the former Midland station – Stamford (Town). Passenger, and indeed the goods services to Bourne had ceased some years earlier in June 1951. The passenger workings on the Bourne route had motive power supplied by New England shed with both New England and Bourne crews sharing the seven return services – curtailed to four during the war years – running over the route up to closure of the line. Ex – GNR tender engines were used, the same engine working an early morning goods train from Peterborough prior to taking on the passenger service. The Bourne route had opened for business in May 1860 and was worked from the outset by the GN with six return passenger trains plying to and from Essendine each weekday, with one on a Sunday. The Bourne & Essendine Railway was absorbed by the GNR in 1864 and, from 1872 a passenger service between Essendine and Sleaford became possible over the line opened in 1871 between Bourne and Sleaford. The N5 is No.69262, another of the batch of six-coupled tanks allocated to New England specifically to work the Stamford-Essendine line in its latter months as a going concern.

Just before we leave Essendine station behind, and consigned to history, we see one of the southbound main line passenger services stopping on 16th May 1959. At its head is a rather scruffy No.60047 DONOVAN, which was to enter Doncaster works within a few days for a General overhaul, from which it emerged with a double chimney. This stopping train was probably one of its last workings prior to that shopping; note the difference in its appearance here to the view, earlier in this album, when it was working an Up express at Peterborough. In the background, beyond the railway boundary, the open field appears to be storing a vast quantity of equipment which is either agricultural or military in origin.

Stamford, Lincolnshire, population 11,120 as at 1950. Ninety-three miles from London and possessing two railway stations, Stamford (Town, from 1950 to 1966) built by the Midland Railway in 1848, and Stamford (East, 1950 to closure), terminus of the Great Northern Railway (S&ER) branch from Essendine, and opened in 1856. This is the terminal station circa 1955 with C12 No.67376 at the head of an early afternoon service to Essendine. The Atlantic tank would have performed this duty many times during its long life having been allocated to New England shed from coming into traffic in 1901. The only time the continuity was broken occurred between May 1946 and January 1951 when it transferred to Hornsey. New England kept the C12 active until it made a final journey to Doncaster in May 1958; on the 22nd of that month it was condemned and shortly afterwards cut up. Note the River Welland flowing along the northern boundary of the railway. This river provided most of the water for the branch engines at Stamford for more than 100 years. BR closed the station on 4th March 1957 and the Essendine trains were then diverted into Stamford (Town) station until the branch closed.

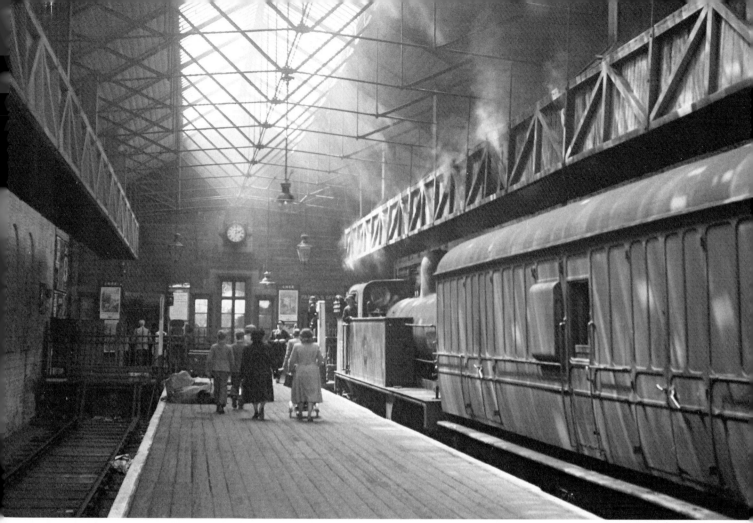

The interior of the station in September 1954 shortly after the arrival of a train from Essendine. The clock reveals the time to be 2.00 p.m. as passengers make their way to the exit. On the walls are various notices, some headed with the BR logo whilst two others still carry LNER above the BR printed posters advertising destinations in far-off corners of the country. Gas lamps abound, as was the case at most BR stations during this period; I wonder if Stamford East station ever got the miracle of electricity fitted? With its stained smoke troughs and smoky ambience, the station was similar to an engine shed.

The rather imposing and somewhat grandiose station building erected by the S&E at Stamford. This is the view in September 1954 when the station was approaching its centenary, and its imminent closure. Today the building, after much refurbishment, houses a number of up-market apartments – very far removed from its original function.

Stamford engine shed 8th September 1954 with C12s Nos.67389 and 67365 being the two branch engines working on this Wednesday. The engine shed dates from 1856 when the Stamford & Essendine Railway were required at night to accommodate the motive power working the branch. The branch engines usually did a two-week stint at Stamford before returning to New England for the necessary maintenance. In the background, beyond the signal box, we can see the overall roof of the station. The connection to the Midland line was opposite the signal box whilst the line to Essendine was to the left of 67389 and its posing crew. Just beyond that is the line which once served the Wansford branch.

**Back on the ECML we meet BR Standard 9F No.92197 running through Corby Glen station with an Up freight on Saturday 3rd October 1959. Everything was still in full bloom including the platform garden plots, the British Isles enjoying something of an Indian summer! However, this station closed on Monday 15th June 1959 but, for all intents and purposes, it appears to be still operational! The two figures on the Up platform are two young boys who were apparently trainspotting and may well have been trespassing but the station name signs and information signs are still in situ. The station had gone through three different names during its 107 years of existence. Initially called simply Corby by the GNR, the name stuck until 1937 when the suffix Lincs. was added. In 1947 it was renamed Corby Glen in time for nationalisation. The signal box dates from 1912 and replaced an older box displaced by station improvements.**

*N.E.Preedy*

We have reached High Dyke, some 101 miles from King's Cross and it's downhill all the way to Grantham from here. It is August 1957 and a southbound Leeds (Central)-King's Cross express rushes past the ironstone exchange siding with one of Copley Hill's Peppercorn A1s in charge. Very soon the Pacific will enter the half mile long Stoke tunnel and emerge into the cutting with the 100 mile marker, en route to Peterborough. Meanwhile, before continuing our journey north it is worth having a look at the wagons in these Down side sidings. Destined mainly for the steelworks centred on Scunthorpe, all of the steel bodied wagons carry iron ore. Note how lightly loaded the wagons appear compared with similar mineral wagons conveying coal for instance; the much denser iron ore required a lot less space, ton for ton. Nevertheless some wagons contain some fairly hefty lumps. Both Grantham and Frodingham sheds shared the iron ore traffic, the former establishment supplying O2s as motive power whilst the Scunthorpe shed relied on its large stud of reliable WD 2-8-0s. Crews changed over at roughly the half way point – empties southbound, loaded northbound. The rear of the express has just passed the signal box which marks the point where the empty wagon sidings stretch off northward. Today these sidings are but a memory, imported ore keeping the blast furnaces of our somewhat dwindling steel industry going, for now.

This B1 is managing to produce a decent smoke screen as it rushes away from Great Ponton towards the capital with the afternoon fish train from Hull in August 1960. No.61075 was a 34A based engine and was hopefully keeping to time as the contents of the vans would not take kindly to the August temperatures. Having worked to Hull on the previous evening with an express freight, the B1 was half way to completing the second leg of its out and back cycle. The fish traffic handled by BR was in something of a decline at this time and by 1964 a total of twenty-five trains were run daily, many lightly loaded to less than fifteen vans. This train loaded about twenty-five vans on this date but was one of a dwindling number sent out from Hull each day. In 1952 the port of Hull alone sent out a dozen fish trains each weekday except Monday when fourteen were loaded. On Saturdays ten trains were handled. BR were finding the fish trade was not to its liking and in a bid to get rid of the traffic in 1964 it proposed that the fish trade accept block trains of the catch be worked to central distribution points from where road transport could take over. The merchants of Hull were not to be messed about and formed their own distribution organisation – using road haulage. The BR contract was ripped up resulting in a loss of half a million pounds to BR revenue!

*D.H.Beecroft*

Great Ponton station, between High Dyke and Grantham, was located at the northern end of the cutting linking the railway to High Dyke sidings. The station itself was sited east of the settlement of the same name, a choice of two lanes, north and west of the station joined the A1 trunk road to the Roman road known as both High Dike and Ermine Street. The place was full of history, the railway station itself dating from 1852. However, history caught up with the passenger station and closure took place on 15th September 1958. On Tuesday 4th August 1959 Thompson A2 No.60500 EDWARD THOMPSON runs down the gradient towards Grantham with a northbound express believed to be *THE HEART OF MIDLOTHIAN.*　　　　*T.G.Hepburn/RAS*

A2 No.60503 **LORD PRESIDENT** appears to be making light work of a heavy Up express as it passes through Great Ponton on the climb to Stoke summit. The date is still 4th August 1959, nearly one year after the station closure, but the goods yard, or at least the section dealing with the local coalmen, is still busy whilst the passenger platforms are deserted except for the weeds getting a grip between the cobbles. The station was best described as 'mean' offering little comfort to the traveller. *T.G.Hepburn/RAS*

**Later the same day our old friend FLYING SCOTSMAN runs in from the north with the 12.30 p.m. Leeds-King's Cross express. With steam to spare, it seems, the fireman throws on another round of coal ready for the both the climb and the race down to Peterborough.**

*T.G.Hepburn/RAS*

**Shortly after completing its penultimate General overhaul, Retford O2/4 No.63945 works a southbound pick-up goods through Great Ponton in mid-August 1959.**

*Peter Groom*

Almost at Grantham now. V2 No.60903 rushes past the water tank at Spitalgate after running beneath the bridge carrying the Great North Road. The date is early September 1959 and the immaculate King's Cross V2 is working Up to King's Cross one of the season's last trains running under *THE SCARBOROUGH FLYER* title. Except for its first three years in traffic spent at Doncaster Carr shed, this engine was at 34A for much of its life until January 1963 when, pre-empting its sister engines at King's Cross, it transferred to New England; by February it was condemned and in May it was taken into Doncaster works for cutting up. 34A was still operational – just!

*D.H.Beecroft*

This is York B16 No.61436, one of the engines as built for the North Eastern Railway in the final month of its final year of existence, and classified B16/1 after some of the class were rebuilt from the 1930s. We have no date for this visit but early 1956 would not be unreasonable because the engine appears to have the last vestiges of a Darlington repaint – after a 'General' – beneath that layer of grime. Unlike us, the B16 appears to be leaving Grantham and is waiting to ring off shed to take on an Up working!

At virtually the same position on the shed yard as the B16, C1 No.62822 is also waiting to go off shed but on a northbound working. This engine started its working life from Grantham shed in 1905 and, as fate would have it, it was to end its life working from Grantham once again. Shortly after Grouping, in June 1924, and as LNER No.3294, the 4-4-2 transferred to New England for a stay which lasted twenty-two years and one day! Boston then got its services from 9th June 1946 until it transferred back to Grantham on 5th January 1947. This engine was one of only two in the class which got BR numbers applied, No.62885 of Darnall being the other. No.62822 was however unique in being the only C1 to carry a smokebox number plate and, apparently, the only one to have a shed plate fitted. Condemned 27th November 1950, No.62822 was the last of its class and went out with a final flourish, working a special train from King's Cross to Doncaster non-stop on the 26th November.

D3 No.62000 on Grantham shed yard in 1950. Under the orders of Edward Thompson, this engine had been given special treatment in 1944 in order to haul Officers saloons and special trains over the LNER. From a General overhaul ending 14th October 1944, it emerged from Doncaster carrying the number 1 but then a week later it was renumbered again becoming 2000. Less than a week after that event it was back in works for a repaint which saw it come out in this lined green livery, ready for its new duties. During the period when it was undergoing the 'General' it had new cab side sheets fitted and these incorporated two windows on each side with hinged glass sight screens positioned between each pair. A brass cap was fitted to the chimney and a coat-of-arms hand painted between the N and E on the tender. A boiler with Ramsbottom safety valves was on the loco at this time. The final retro step was to replace its Group Standard buffers with the original GNR type. In October 1947 LNER was restored to the tender, the crest remaining in position, and another boiler, this time with Ross pop valves fitted. From a Casual Light repair, the D3 came out of Doncaster in January 1950 with its BR number and the small BR emblem where the crest had been. The LNER had been crudely – for Doncaster – painted over and the letters are still visible in this illustration. The 4-4-0 went for scrap in October 1951.

The Down bay platform at the north end of Grantham station had two faces as illustrated in this Wednesday 23rd July 1958 photograph with J6 No.64249 heading a three-coach non-gangwayed set which was making up an afternoon stopping service to Nottingham. To the left of the picture, stabled in the Up side bay platform, is a diesel multiple unit on a Lincoln service which was one of the first local services on the Eastern Region to be dieselised. For all its importance Grantham station is still unchanged from GNR days, with gas lamps holding their own in a rapidly changing world of modernisation. In the right background stands the original four-road shed (old or Bottom shed) which by now was roofless and was eventually abandoned by the Motive Power Department through lack of maintenance. Luckily Grantham had another engine shed (new or Top shed) a little way down the yard to the south of the older structure. That sufficed for the remaining few years of Grantham's locomotive requirements.

Station pilot for the day on Saturday 11th April 1959 was N2 No.69516. A relative newcomer to the Grantham allocation, having transferred from Hornsey on 16th November 1958, the N2 had spent most of its life working from sheds situated in London, including eleven years at Stratford, and more than two years at Neasden besides nine years at Hatfield. During the formative years of the LNER it also worked in Scotland for five years. Now it was working its passage back to Doncaster - slowly. A victim of dieselisation and no longer required at the southern end of the ECML, the six-coupled tank still had some use and was given to Grantham for duties such as these which were once the preserve of C12 tanks. Eventually, though, dieselisation caught up and No.69516 made a final journey to Doncaster, and oblivion, being broken up there in early 1961.

A much brighter day on 4th August 1958 reveals this busy scene at Grantham with C12 No.67367 working as pilot and dividing a train with an 0-6-0 tender engine at the south end. In between the engines the train comprises a couple of articulated units, a brake third and a Gresley full brake. New England V2 No.60875, working empty carriage stock, has pulled up alongside the water column serving the through goods lines. Later in the month the V2 would be en route to Darlington works to have AWS fitted. We are possibly witnessing one of the final duties undertaken by the C12 before it attended Doncaster 'Plant' because on Friday 8th August, as it arrived in works, it was condemned.

**MALLARD** takes over the Up *FLYING SCOTSMAN* from **BITTERN** at Grantham circa 1953. Note that No.60022 is carrying the LNER pre-war painted version of the headboard which by now looks rather tired. No.60019 however has the British Railways version with THE prefix and circular plaques showing the entwined rose and thistle. A Gateshead engine since 1943, No.60019 is reversing along the Down fast line to gain entry to the engine shed from the north end of the station whilst MALLARD has coupled up to the train for the last dash to London. No longer a non-stop express, *THE FLYING SCOTSMAN* would have changed engines at Newcastle and, as witnessed, here at Grantham. This regular changeover at that time was a magnet for the young and not-so-young enthusiasts of Grantham, the Newcastle-Grantham working often bringing something rare to the town. During BR days several changes were made to engine workings on both Up and Down services with Newcastle and often Grantham, too, being engine change points.

**Waiting at the south end of the station to take a southbound express onwards to King's Cross, Grantham shedded A3 No.60046 DIAMOND JUBILEE is lamped-up and ready for the job in hand. This is an A3 in its final form with AWS and trough type smoke deflectors.**

Standing at virtually the same position as DIAMOND JUBILEE, Thompson A2/1 No.60508 DUKE OF ROTHESAY awaits a southbound working at an unknown date. It carries a 35A New England shed plate but note the reversed train headboard on the lower centre lamp iron – the legend painted on its surface reads 'Return to Peterborough Loco'. The lamp irons themselves are unusual and were fitted to accept an electric lighting system that was intended for but never fitted to the Pacific when built (as No.3697) and instead found its way to No.4470 GREAT NORTHERN!

We are now at the north end of Grantham station with Heaton A3 No.60091 CAPTAIN CUTTLE waiting to take a Down express off to Newcastle. The date is unknown but the Pacific carries a 52B shedplate and it was allocated to Heaton from June 1948 to July 1958, and from September 1962 to June 1963. The latter date range can be discarded because it has neither AWS, smoke deflectors or double chimney, and the BR emblem still adorns the tender side. Therefore, anywhere up to July 1957 would be acceptable because it went into works that month for a 'General' and came out with the new BR crest – albeit a wrong-facing version on this side. The presence of the Derby Lightweight d.m.u. in the background would shorten the date span too.

Can you remember what the view from the south end of Grantham station platforms looked like in steam days? Well here is a reminder – fantastic isn't it. This is Thursday 17th July 1958 with A3 No.60104 SOLARIO heading an afternoon Down express. Carriage sidings to the right, goods facilities to the left. Out of sight to the right of course were the two engine sheds complete with coaling plant, coaling stage, water softener and the unique scissors triangle created to turn locomotives in the absence of a turntable. Have you visited Grantham recently? The trains run faster it seems, there are more of them too, but they are somewhat shorter. Gaze out from the station platforms, south, west and north. Something radical has taken place in the fifty-three years since this scene was captured. With hindsight it appears that we were lucky enough to have seen our railway system at its zenith – admitted a rather rundown one – but nevertheless it was the steam railway. We managed to see it all before it collapsed into the streamlined and somewhat heartless business it is today. Variety is the spice? It sure was.

Lets have a look around Grantham engine shed now. We are in the yard of the 'New' or, as it was also known at Grantham 'the Top shed'. The date once again escapes us but early to mid 1950s is a reasonable guess, certainly before January 1954 when it acquired a lipped chimney in Doncaster Works. Thompson A2/3 No.60518 TEHRAN is polluting the atmosphere but the fire had to be built up somehow. The Gateshead based Pacific is getting ready to work home and its driver – note the white collar, tie and polished footwear – is having a look around whilst the fireman peers down from the cab. Grantham's illustrious history as a major locomotive changing point was drawing to a close but scenes such as this carried on until September 1963 when it finally ceased after 108 years. The roll call of Pacifics allocated to Grantham shed during the LNER and BR period was indeed impressive – basically every class except the Thompson A2/1 and A2/2 had graced its rails, even the one-off A1/1 managed a six year residence.

From any angle the Peppercorn A1 was impressive looking. No.60128 BONGRACE – I wonder what visitors to these shores made of such names when noticed – moves off shed to take on a Down working. Scenes like this were re-enacted dozens of times every day with a kind of permanence attached to them. However, progress, like time, marches on and eventually what appears to be permanent will end. And so it did at Grantham and hundreds of other sheds around the country during a decade of wanton destruction carried out in the name of progress.

Back to the station on that changeable 11th April 1959 Saturday. Working a southbound freight along the Up main is a nicely turned out Thompson B1 No.61179 of King's Cross shed. The schoolboy walking down the platform may not appear to be interested but we can be fairly sure why this engine was working this train on this particular day. Clues to the answer lay in the appearance of the twelve year old engine. Beneath that recent coat of dirt is a repainted B1 courtesy of Doncaster paint shop. No.61179 had just completed a General overhaul (19th February to 26th March) and after all its post-repair mechanical checks had been carried out and running-in completed, it was time to release the B1 back into traffic. How to get it home? Work it light engine – expensive and non-revenue earning; put it on a passenger working – all of those were already diagrammed for Pacifics and V2s; put it on a goods train of sorts and it will eventually work south – reasonable and not too strenuous. But note that 61179 is showing the lamp code of a pick-up goods! It would be interesting to know how long it took this engine to complete the Doncaster-King's Cross journey. 115

Later in the day and during a shower, Colwick K3 No.61914 rumbles into Grantham with an Up mineral train bound for New England yards. Towards the back end of the train, just past the signal box, can be seen a receding d.m.u. – were they camera shy or did railway photographers tend to ignore them?

Changeable weather indeed. It is late in the afternoon of 11th April 1959 now. The warm air has cleared the residue of the earlier rain shower and the enthusiasts are once again able to stretch their legs. Meanwhile this Copley Hill V2, No.60885, is waiting for the off signal with a Leeds working.

Thursday morning, 20th August 1959, it's warm and sunny. People are on holiday from both work and school. Day trips are in order and this family waiting on the Up platform are optimistically dressed in lightweight summer clothing. Their idle chatter is silenced momentarily whilst they observe the passing of Retford O2/4 No.63924 working a southbound mineral train towards New England. A nice scene summing up an era long gone.

Remember the view earlier which featured the vista from the south end of Grantham station with A3 No.60104 SOLARIO approaching on that Down express? Well, here is the equivalent vista at the north end on Wednesday 23rd July 1958. It appears to be early afternoon with hazy sun and hopefully it was warm though the figure leaning against the lamp post on the right would have us believe otherwise. On the far right a diesel multiple unit is departing from the north end, Up side bay platform on a Lincoln service whilst L1 No.67800 (the last to be built) arrives with a pick-up from the Nottingham line. The tank wagons in the siding on the left appear in many of the photographs taken at this end of the station no matter what year they were taken. In the right foreground we can see the 'white' tiles lining the wall of the public subway (No.242) which ran beneath the station at this location; the footbridge linking the platforms was No.241 in the Civil Engineer's list of 'under and over line structures', whilst Springfield Road bridge was No.240.

Peppercorn A2 No.60526 SUGAR PALM was leaning into the curve as it rejoined the main line with an Up express at Barkston South Junction following an ECML traffic diversion through western Lincolnshire. The date is 2nd June 1957 – a Sunday. In the left background an O2 heads an Engineers train which will have been serving the works responsible for the re-routing. Barkston junction was of course well known for being the turnaround point where many locomotives on running-in turns, after overhaul at Doncaster Plant works, would traverse the triangle in order to head northwards chimney first. *T.G.Hepburn/RAS*

**Peppercorn A1 No.60143 SIR WALTER SCOTT, runs through the staggered platform station at Barkston with a Down express on that second day of June 1957. As can be seen from the signals, the train is diverting to the east. Opening rather late, 1867, for an ECML wayside station, Barkston was closed a bit earlier than most on 7th February 1955.**

*T.G.Hepburn/RAS*

Obviously taken on 'diversion Sunday,' this photograph shows to advantage the Down platform at Barkston whilst another express, headed by V2 No.60928, rejoins the main line from the wilds of Lincolnshire. Besides this platform on the main line, Barkston also had a Down platform on the Lincoln line but that was closed before British Railways came into being.

*T.G.Hepburn/RAS*

**Newark South Junction, 16th June 1958. Heading a nine-coach Up express, A3 No.60054 PRINCE OF WALES passes a stationary goods train loaded with agricultural tractors. The long freight, hauled by WD No.90421, is standing on the former Great Northern/London & North Western Joint line from Bottesford and is awaiting the passage of a northbound express before proceeding onto the Down main. The origin of the tractors and indeed their eventual destination is unknown.** *J.Foreman*

An early morning shed-bash hits Newark engine shed on a glorious Saturday 3rd April 1954. A member of staff, probably a senior driver on light-duties, is looking after the place and the visiting party. Newark was a sub-shed of Retford at this time and was to remain so up to closure on 5th January 1959. Its engines were supplied by Retford, even the three former Midland tanks – an 0-6-0T for shunting Newark (Castle) station, and two 0-4-4T for the Southwell branch – came under the control of 36E. One the Southwell engines, No.58085, is foremost is this view. Note the ex GCR flavour of the other engines in the picture, J11 No.64423 and an N5 poking out of the shed. The GN was represented by the J52, No.68863, which was behind the J11, and a J6 No.64234 inside the shed. Other residents on that day were Nos.58077, 64341, 64403, 69282, 69283, and 69300. The aforementioned driver looks toward the camera with a resigned look and was probably wondering what this coach party of 'civilians' were doing upsetting an otherwise normal spring morning.

The ECML was blighted by a couple of flat crossings south of Doncaster. The GN/GC crossing at Retford was eventually eliminated when BR constructed a burrowing junction beneath the ECML in the mid-1960s, the expenditure being necessary to allow an increase in coal traffic to the newly opened Trent Valley power stations. However, the crossing at Newark, highlighted here by the passage of Stanier Cl.4 No.42587 working a Nottingham-Lincoln passenger service across the ECML in June 1963, is still in situ. Its traffic levels are such that a flyover or dive-under (the nearby presence of the River Trent must make the latter option the least favoured) is still not a requirement. The advances in signalling must also favour this junction for some decades to come.

*D.H.Beecroft*

Turning his camera 180 degrees on that same June day in 1963, the photographer captured King's Cross A4 No.60008 DWIGHT D. EISENHOWER crossing the Trent bridge at Newark with an Up express, whilst another express crossed the river bridge in the northbound direction. On its front end the Pacific carries a legend in chalk which suggests the imminent end of steam workings. To some extent that was true for the section of the ECML south of Peterborough and especially King's Cross engine shed which closed that month. No.60008 was transferred to New England on 16th June but a month later it was withdrawn before eventually being shipped to the United States in 1964 for preservation. As for the prophecy - well, so far, so good.

*D.H.Beecroft*

New England 9F No.92187 runs over Muskham water troughs on 25th July 1959 whilst working a Down Leeds express. Just eighteen months old, this filthy example was nonetheless mechanically sound. Meanwhile BR were still building additional 9Fs.

*D.H.Beecroft* 127

A superb view of the junction and interchange sidings at Tuxford Junction on Saturday 10th August 1957 with Peppercorn A1 No.60133 POMMERN heading the Down *QUEEN OF SCOTS* towards its first stop at Leeds (Central). On the bridge in the background a passenger train from the Lincoln direction heads west and is passing the point where the former LD&ECR high level station - Dukeries Junction - had recently been demolished (the Great Northern had their own station at the lower level beneath the bridge; both stations closed in 1950). Today, that bridge and the railway it carries, is still in situ albeit with no traffic since the link to Lincoln was severed and the base load power station at High Marnham was closed. *N.E.Preedy*

Tuxford, Sunday 24th May 1959. We are now looking north from the same public road bridge used to capture the scene in the previous illustration. A rather grotty looking A3, No.60066 MERRY HAMPTON, of King's Cross, is working south with the 10.35 a.m. Leeds-King's Cross. Towards the rear of the train is the closed GNR station formerly known as Tuxford (North) which was opened in 1852 and closed in July 1955. The level crossing beyond the station catered for the road traffic on the A611. Seemingly growing out of the locomotive's double chimney is a nice example of GNR concrete signal post.

**Tuxford some three years later. It is Monday 18th June 1962 and looking north again, we are this time on the surviving Down platform of the former GN station. The ECML motive power does not appear to have got any cleaner during the intervening years, even for prestige working like** *THE YORKSHIRE PULLMAN* **but this Copley Hill A1, No.60120 KITTIWAKE, may well have been a stand-in for a failed diesel locomotive.**

*David Dalton*

**Just north of Tuxford was East Markham where the A57 trunk road crossed the ECML via a level crossing. This classic shot of a main line express shows A3 No.60039 SANDWICH with a King's Cross-Newcastle express entering the cutting on the afternoon of Sunday 15th June 1958. The lone tree could one day present a hazard to passing trains but just now it adds to the scene.** *N.E.Preedy*

It wasn't just the during their twilight years that the A4s were pressed into freight service – Scotch Goods aside. This is a rather dirty No.60016 SILVER KING working north through Askham tunnel with a fitted freight on Sunday 8th July 1956. The Pacific wasn't en route to Doncaster Plant for overhaul as might be assumed, it was in fact one of the Gateshead engines working home which, to some degree, explains the exterior grime.

*N.E.Preedy*

Proceeding further north, we are now one hundred and thirty-seven miles from King's Cross, and have reached the outskirts of Retford, at Grove Road level crossing. It is a glorious sunny afternoon on 24th May 1959 as Doncaster A1 No.60157 GREAT EASTERN passes with the 2.56 p.m. Leeds-King's Cross consisting thirteen vehicles. Level crossings have long been a nuisance to the railway – road users would echo that sentiment but for a different reason – and even today on the electrified ECML there are still dozens requiring the complete attention of the signalling staff. Within a ten mile radius of Retford there are more than twenty level crossings, including this one at Grove Road.

We are now at Retford and the first sight that greets us is this BR Standard 9F clattering over the crossing and points at the south end of the station. No.92186 has charge of a northbound express on Saturday 2nd September 1961. The spotters on the platform would have been none too pleased to see a goods engine where a 'namer' should have been, likewise, the powers-that-be would presumably have been less than pleased too. However, with locomotive shortages and failures occurring during a summer timetable weekend, the Motive Power Department probably had no choice but to employ the ten-coupled 9F; after all, cancellations were frowned upon more than employing the 'wrong' engines in those days. Besides, the 9F was quite capable of fast running and the crews didn't seem to mind at all, some actually relishing the task to see what kind of speeds they could get out of their charge – 90 m.p.h. was recorded with No.92184 south of Grantham in August 1958 whilst working an Up Edinburgh express. The 2-10-0 illustrated was one of New England's batch on this date and probably worked as far as York. For the record, No.92184 and 92187 were also New England based.

**The more usual fare served up for express working. Doncaster based A1 No.60119 PATRICK STIRLING heads north with a Down express circa summer 1962.**

135

Crossing the ECML by way of the station subway, we are now on the Up platform at Retford, at the point where the platform curves eastward towards the alignment of the former GCR Sheffield to Lincoln route. However, the actual platform did not reach all the way round to where this spur physically joins the west-east main line. Also on that September 1961 Saturday which witnessed the 9F express working, one of Lincoln's batch of K3, No.61848, stops with a Lincoln bound service from an unknown source. What is known is that the scruffy K3 has just over one year of operational life left before it was called into Doncaster for cutting up.

Moving along to the north end of the same platform on that Saturday 2nd September 1961, we come across Thompson B1 No.61225 performing a bit of shunting in the Up sidings. This is the point where the loop from Whisker Hill junction joins the ECML to enable passenger trains to and from Sheffield to use the station platforms. The road bridge spanning the loop line is just visible between the array of signals at the end of the Down platform. Looking at the main line signals in the background, it appears that a southbound non-stop train is due through any minute.

Remaining at the north end of the station but crossing over to the Down platform, and going back in time, we come across this Ivatt Atlantic No.2817 at the head of a Sheffield train. Although it appears that we have receded too far back in time to the pre-Nationalisation period, we haven't. This is 1950 – Tuesday 11th April to be precise – and the days of this Darnall based C1 are numbered. Its last works visit had taken place during March and April 1947; hence the LNER still adorning the tender, and it was due another visit to Doncaster very soon. On Monday 8th May 1950, twenty-seven days after this scene was captured on film, this Large Atlantic was condemned at Doncaster works. One of seventeen which became BR property, No.2817 was the penultimate locomotive in service; the last was No.62822 as previously mentioned, which remained operational until November 1950.

On the west side of the station was the former GNR engine shed which was a dead-end building recently rebuilt at the time of this 19th September 1954 photograph. Left to right the three occupants poking out of the doorways were B1 No.61208, N5 No.69313 and O4 No.63637. Simply because of the engines on view you could be forgiven for thinking this was the former GCR shed which was situated about a half mile to the east, on the south side of the GC line. That place, or at least its yard, was usually full of ex GN O2 goods engines. BR treated the two separate engine sheds at Retford as one establishment hence the mingling of the pre-Group allocations. The doors at this place are having a coat of paint, a rare event at any BR engine shed during this period but here we have it caught on camera. Perhaps the painting of the doors was the culmination of the shed rebuilding which started in 1951.

Gracing the GN shed yard on 30th April 1962 was O2 No.63924, one of the original GNR engines built by North British Locomotive Co. which was fitted with a side window cab in July 1939. No.63924 had been allocated to Retford since September 1952, having 140 arrived there after a two year stint at Mexborough. We saw this 2-8-0 earlier, working a coal train through Grantham.

An afternoon trip working dawdles through Retford station with J11/3 No.64324 at its head during the early or mid-summer of 1962. The Down line has something 'pegged' and looking at the intending passengers on the platform it may well have been a 'stopper'. Retford certainly kept the enthusiast and photographer busy with expresses, ordinary passenger trains, freight trains of every description and light engine movements galore. For the spotter the best place was the curving platform serving the Lincoln line, this location gave a good view of most train movements; only engine movements off the two depots could evade scrutiny. This particular J11 was a relative newcomer to the Retford allocation, transferring to 36E from Langwith Junction in January 1961, it was kept in work until the end of summer 1962, when it was sent to Gorton works and condemned on 23rd September. During its sixty year life this engine had carried eighteen different boilers, not a record for this class by any means, and more like the average.

We have no date for this photograph but it would be a fair bet to put it down to the same afternoon as the previous illustration. The spotters give us either late afternoon after school has finished or the school holidays. The subject is of course Gresley A4 No.60006 SIR RALPH WEDGWOOD whisking a London bound express along the Up fast. For a King's Cross engine its external appearance doesn't exactly come up to the standard expected of that shed during this period. It may well have been due for a General overhaul because it certainly attended Doncaster from 7th August to 10th October 1962 for such. This A4 was one of the luckier ones in that it found further employment in Scotland after New England had discarded it. The late 1962 overhaul had certainly given it a fighting chance for the following three years.

Another undated photograph featuring a King's Cross A4. This is No.60033 SEAGULL in charge of what is almost certainly the King's Cross-Niddrie (Scotch Goods) fast freight which worked north through Retford at about 6.30 p.m. What we can confirm regarding a date is that it was certainly before the end of April 1961 because on the 22nd of that month the Pacific attended Doncaster works for a General overhaul (out 8th June) at which a speed indicator was fitted on this side of the engine. No.60033 was one of the early casualties of the A4 class and was condemned in December 1962, long before 'Top Shed' was closed.

Whilst we are at Retford it is worth deviating slightly from our south-north course to take a look at Thrumpton engine shed on 19th September 1954. This former Great Central (MS&LR) shed consisted just two covered roads but had a sizeable yard of which every spare yard was taken up at weekends by locomotives stabling after a week of toil hauling coal trains between colliery and railhead. The shed had been rebuilt during the same period that the ex-GN shed had undergone a rebuild and evidence of that undertaking can be seen in the shape of new brickwork atop the original walls. As mentioned earlier, the ex-GC shed was usually full of ex-GN locomotives and to prove the point here is J3 No.64140 stabled alongside the shed (admitted one J3 does not exactly prove anything but the yard at the east end of the shed, as far as the London Road boundary, was crammed with 0-6-0s and 2-8-0s from both denominations). This particular J3 was to be the last of its class. A fairly recent arrival at Retford, No.64140 had transferred from Hitchin on 8th February 1953 after spending nearly twenty years working at the southern end of the ECML. The J3 entered Doncaster works on 22nd December 1954 and was condemned that same day, aged fifty-four years and six months. It was cut up soon afterwards.

144 So concludes Part 2 of our journey. Part 3 will take us onward to Doncaster and York!